Introduction

Long before Mickey, the world already belonged to the mice. In recent years an entirely new species has rapidly spread to every corner of the globe. These are sophisticated, hardworking mice—sleek, smart, and ubiquitous. They cut, they paste, they highlight, they draw pictures. They are sensitive, they snuggle in your hand, and they don't squeak. They click. And you couldn't get much done without yours.

At the end of a grueling session, when your mouse sits vibrating with exhaustion on the pad, it deserves to rest in a mouse house of distinction—something unique, worldly, impressive. What mouse wouldn't find peace in the cosmic interior of India's Taj Mahal or the vaulted chambers of France's Chartres Cathedral? Perhaps your mouse would prefer the classic lines of the Greek Parthenon. A nose for power might suggest a stay at 1600 Pennsylvania Avenue. Or, if a more contemplative existence is preferred, there's Japan's magnificent Golden Pavilion.

In just a few minutes you can lovingly assemble any of these five dramatic residences. All will inspire and restore, providing home and safe haven for your trusty sidekick after those long days spent roaming the far reaches of the electronic frontier.

Building Tips

Although it is not necessary, your mouse house will be sturdier and have a longer life if you tape the tabs down once they are in place. This will also help prevent the tabs from inadvertently pulling out of their slots as you assemble the rest of the building.

All of the mouse house pieces are printed on both sides. In the assembly instructions when we refer to the "underside," we mean the back side, on which no letters appear.

Let the building commence!

Golden Pavilion

Your mouse will be inspired and soothed by the classical Shinden lines of this world-renowned temple.

The extraordinary Tea Room—and more than fifteen other elegant chambers—are all wired for air conditioning and cable. Interior ceilings feature gold leaf in delicate filigree. Pool room in basement.

Includes lake, ideal for meditation, koi fishing.

HOW TO BUILD THE GOLDEN PAVILION

PIECE 1 (lower walls): Fold away from you along all dotted score lines.

PIECE 2 (lower walls): Fold as you did for piece 1. Connect piece 1 to piece 2 by inserting tabs A and B into slots A and B. Connect tabs C, D, E, and F to corresponding slots C, D, E, and F. Secure all connections with tape on underside.

PIECE 3 (eaves over front door): Fold away from you along all five dotted score lines to create two roof eaves. Insert tabs G into slots that surround the door on piece 1.

PIECE 4 (large roof): Fold away from you along all dotted score lines. Align center hole with hole on top of structure. Pull tabs H through slots H in roof until slots I in tabs are visible.

PIECE 5 (second story floor): Line up with square hole. Push tabs I through slots I. Secure with tape on underside.

PIECE 6 (upper walls): Fold away from you along all dotted score lines, except score lines on four golden shapes at top. These should be folded back towards you along the lower slotted score lines, and away from you along score lines above. Insert tabs J, K, L, and M into corresponding slots J, K, L, and M, taping each tab to underside as you go. Insert tab N into slot N and secure with tape on underside. Lock tabs O to each other so that the letters "O" are visible. Lock tabs P to each other so that the letters "P" do not show.

PIECE 7 (small roof): Fold away from you along all dotted score lines. Slide hole in roof down over golden "box" on piece 6, with tabs Q pointing straight down. Push tabs Q through slots Q and secure with tape, one tab at a time, to underside. Connect upper floor assembly to lower floor by pushing tabs R into corner gaps surrounding piece 5. **HINT:** Gently bend up all roof corners to simulate "Shinden" roof line.

PIECE 8 (rooster): Carefully fold one half of split tab toward you, one away. Tuck tabs under the overlaps formed by tabs P on top of building.

PUT MOUSE IN HOUSE.

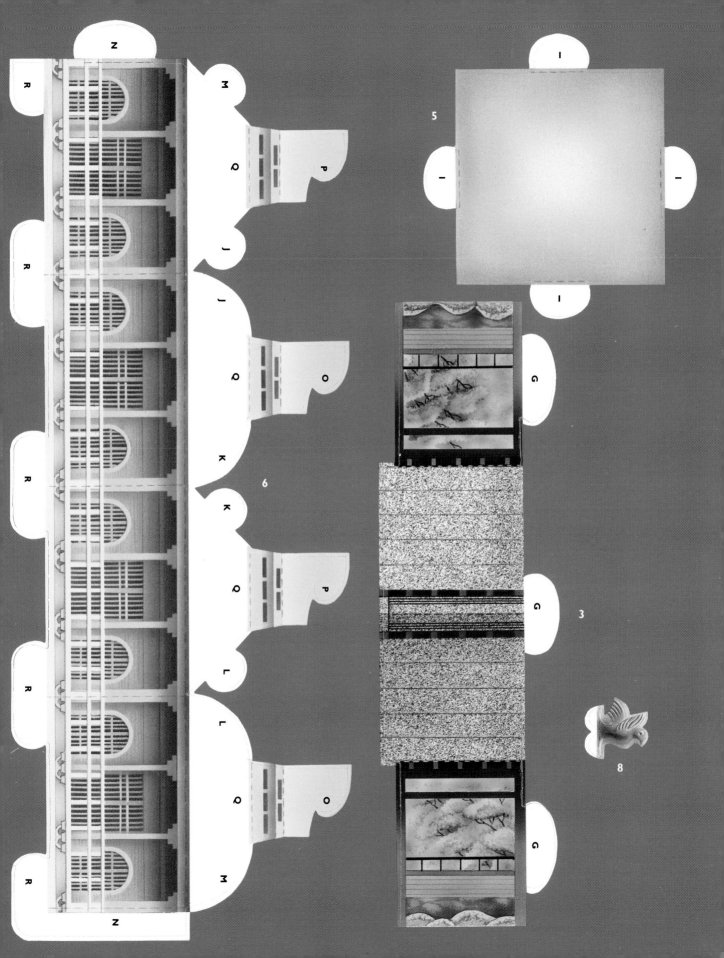

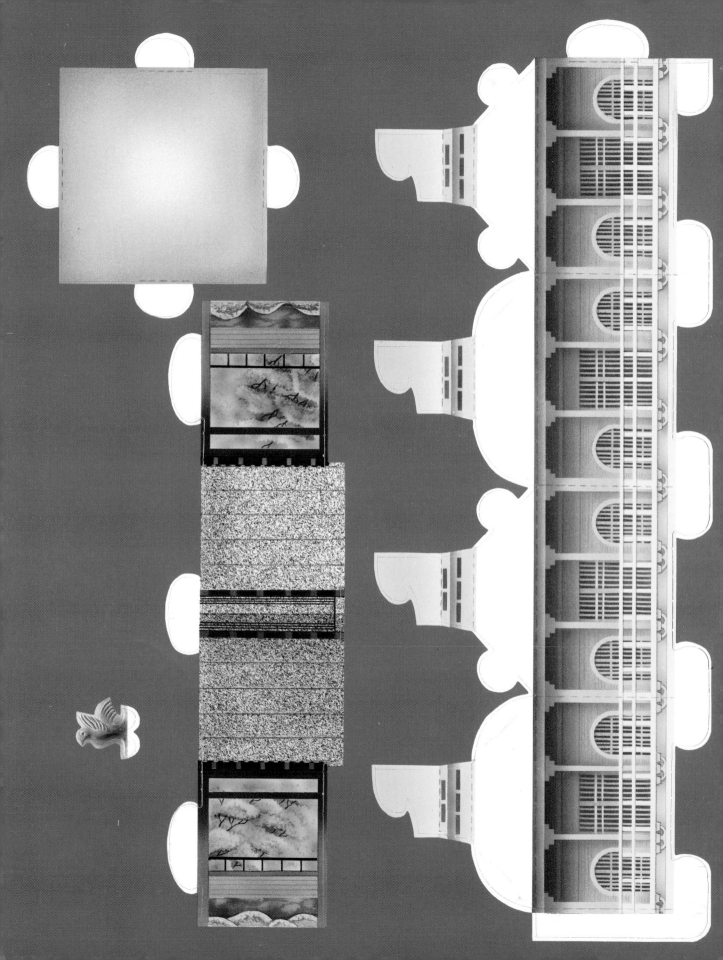

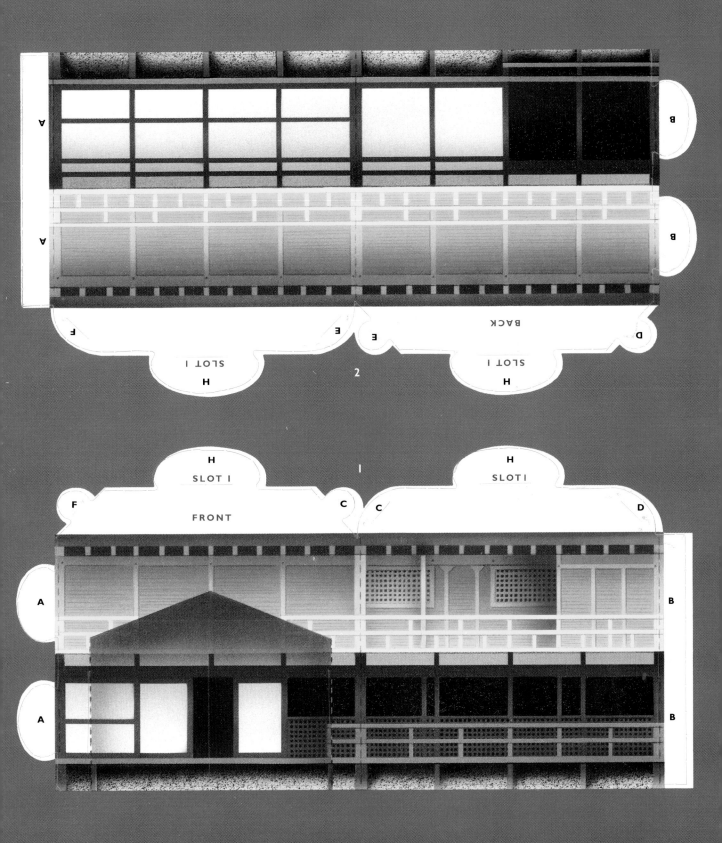

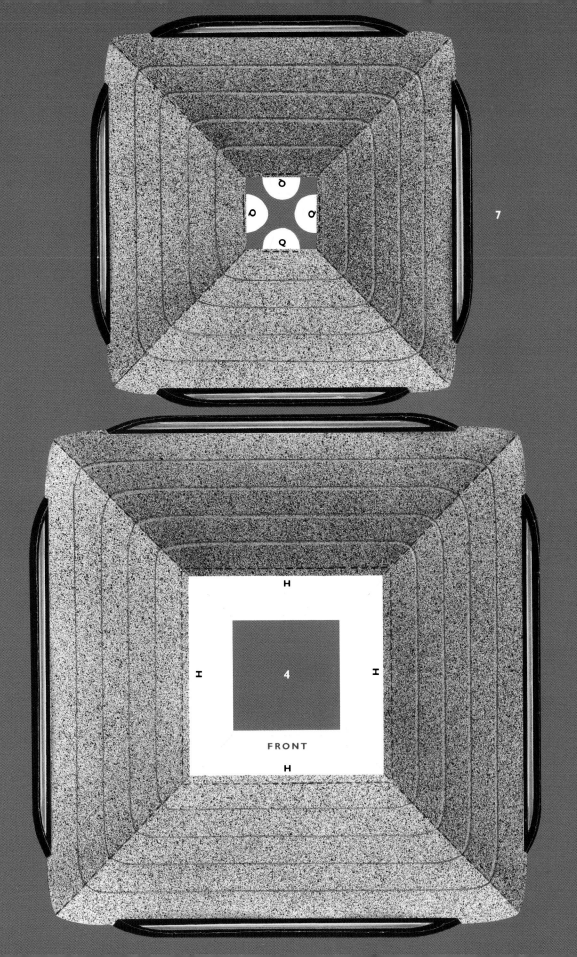

Taj Mahal

After centuries off-market, this truly monumental 17th-century dome-top offers a rare investment opportunity for the discerning mouse. Extensive gardens with over 1,000 species of flora and a dramatic reflecting pool make outdoor entertaining a must. Interior marbled walkways, with exquisite inscriptions and semiprecious stone inlay, make for simple but elegant living.

Ancient craftsmanship meets modern convenience in this brilliantly and beautifully conceived structure. If there's a more uplifting residence, with better acoustics, we haven't found it.

HOW TO BUILD THE TAJ MAHAL

PIECE 1 (dome): Insert tabs A into the semi-circle of slots in piece 2. The shadow on piece 2 should fall behind the dome. Secure tabs in place with tape on underside.

PIECE 2 (roof): Fold away from you along all dotted score lines.

PIECE 3 (back and side walls): Fold away from you along all dotted score lines, except for the uppermost score line on each of the two towers. Fold these towers towards you along these lines.

PIECE 4 (entrance and side walls): Repeat what you did for piece 3. Connect piece 4 to piece 3 by inserting tab B into slot B and tab C into slot C. Next fold corner tabs D behind each tab E and then fold each tab E back under structure. Each letter "E" should be facing downwards. Tape tabs D to inner walls to form a corner brace for each of the four corners.

Gently place dome and roof piece on top of walls, with front of dome oriented to front entrance of building. Push each of the four tower tops up and through the four roof slots. Tuck the edges of the roof inside the walls, and then pull the towers up and push the edges of the roof down—as far as both will go. Tape the roof flaps to the underside of the structure.

PIECE 5 (minaret tower): Fold away from you along the two dotted score lines. Insert tabs F into vertical corner slots on right side of building.

PIECE 6 (minaret tower): Repeat what you did for piece 5 on the other side of the building.

PUT MOUSE IN HOUSE.

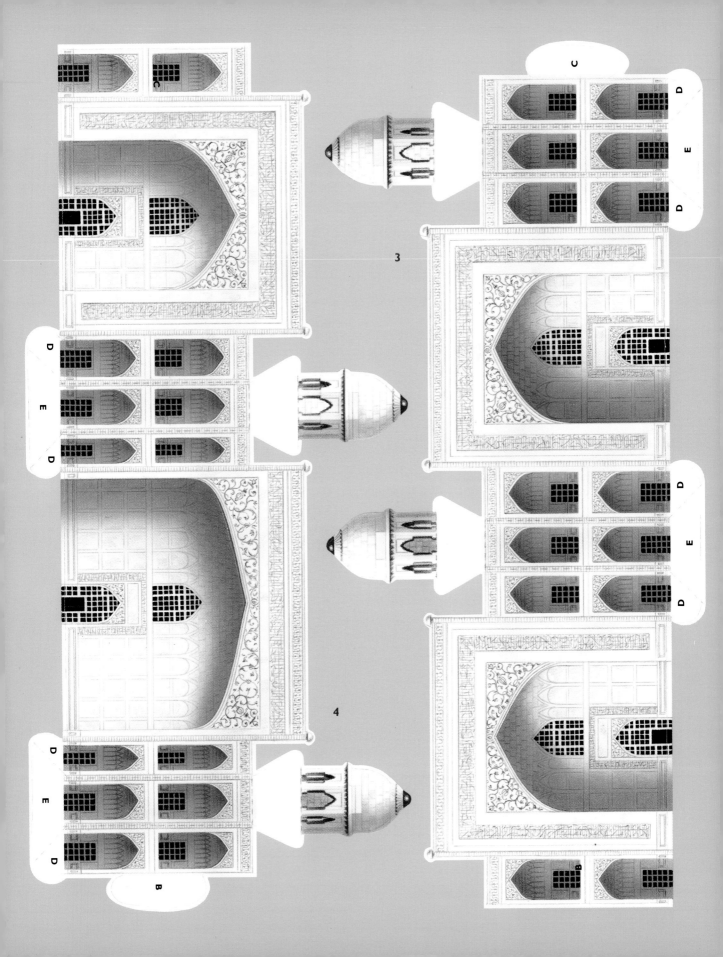

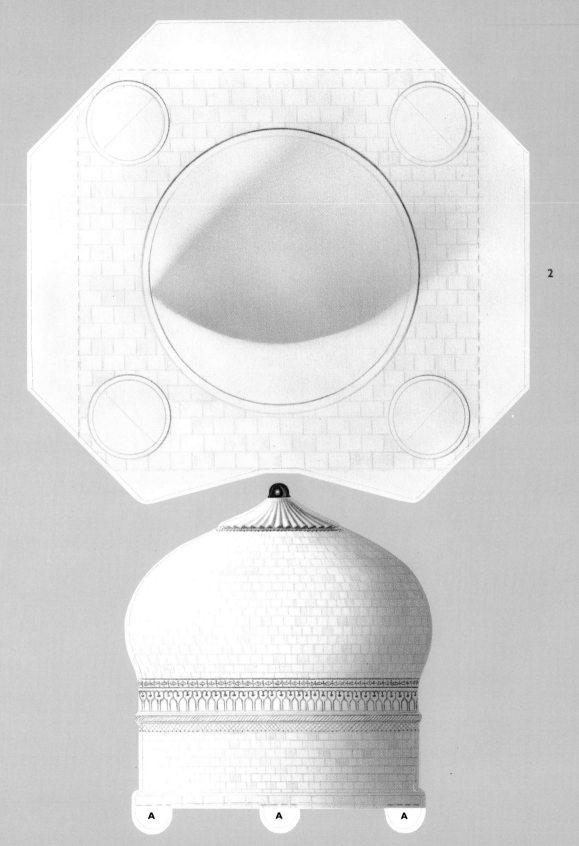

2

A   A   A

1

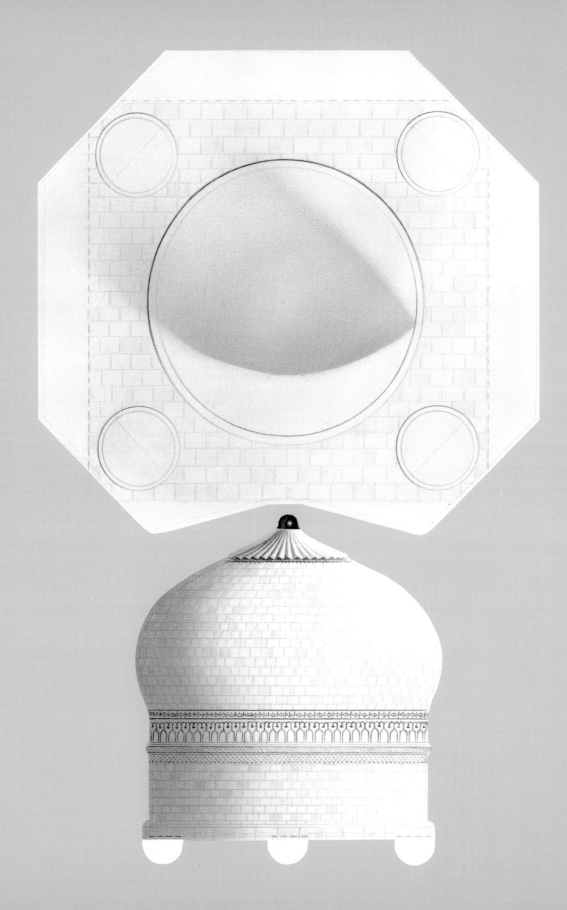

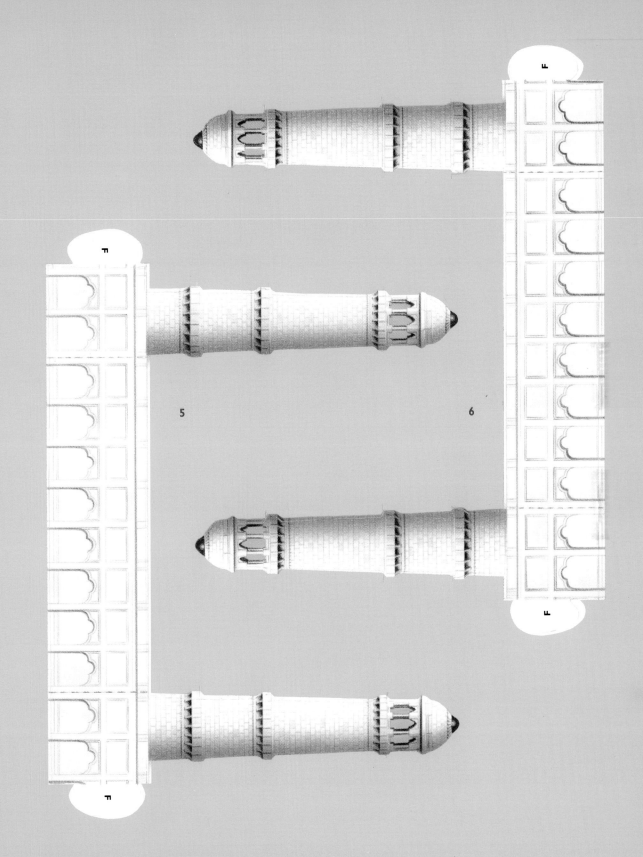

5

6

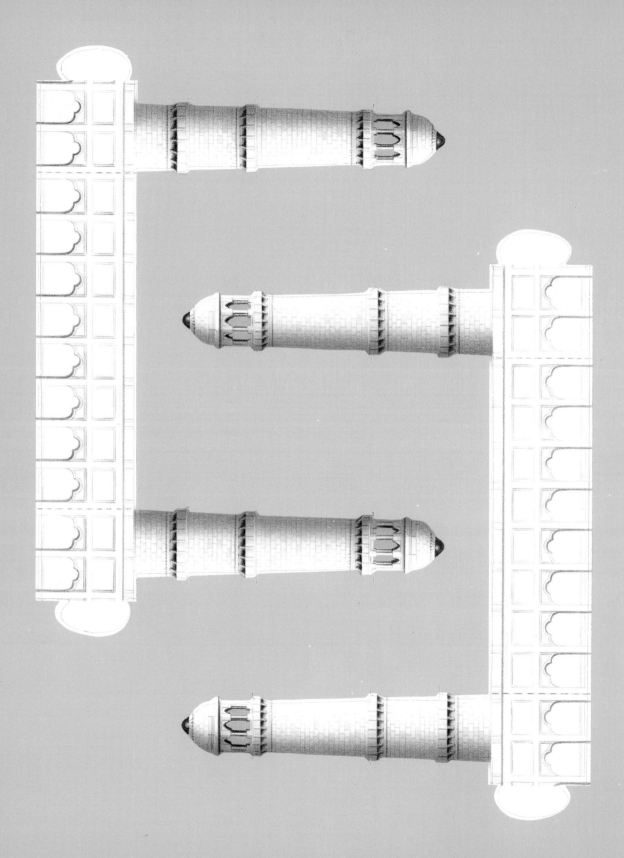

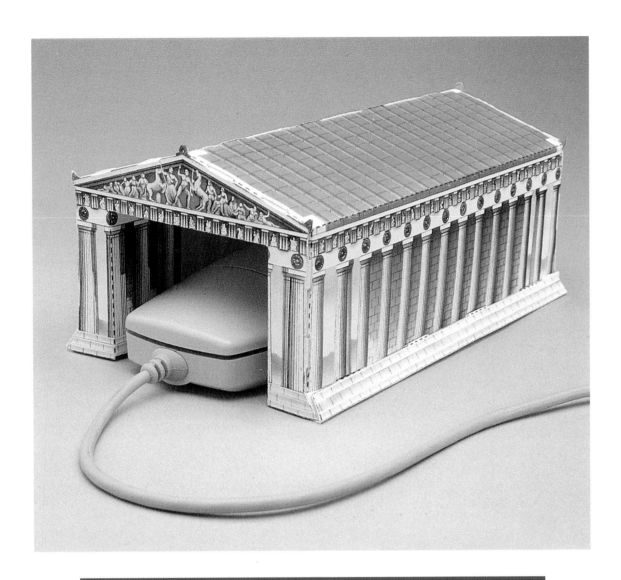

The Parthenon

This fixer-upper offers spectacular views of both Athens and the Aegean. Created by Ictinus & Callicrates, the Golden Era's preeminent design firm, the Parthenon's ideal proportions have set design standards for centuries. Over 500 feet of interior frieze makes this a house that requires little interior decoration.

For the mouse handy with masonry and heavy stone, caring for this classic will be a lifelong labor of love. Note: Offered strictly on an AS IS basis.

HOW TO BUILD THE PARTHENON

PIECE 1 (side and roof): Fold bottom edge up and towards you along both dotted score lines, inserting tabs A into corresponding slots A. Pull tabs all the way into each slot. Fold away from you along all remaining dotted score lines.

PIECE 2 (side and roof): Repeat what you did for piece 1. Then join pieces 1 and 2 at roof top, inserting tabs C into corresponding slots C.

PIECE 3 (front): Fold all tabs away from you. Insert small tabs D into their corresponding slots D on the structure made from pieces 1 and 2. Insert tabs into roof first, securing tabs with tape on underside, and work down from there. Insert tabs E into their respective triangular bases.

PIECE 4 (back): Repeat what you did for piece 3.

PUT MOUSE IN HOUSE.

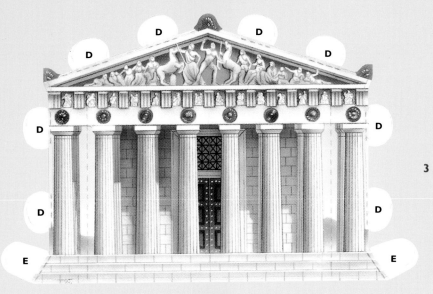

FRONT

3

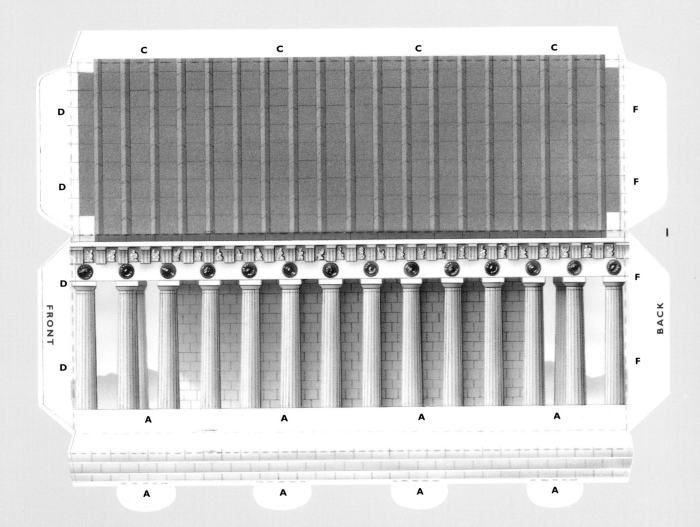

C C C C

D F

D F

I

D F

FRONT BACK

D F

A A A A

A A A A

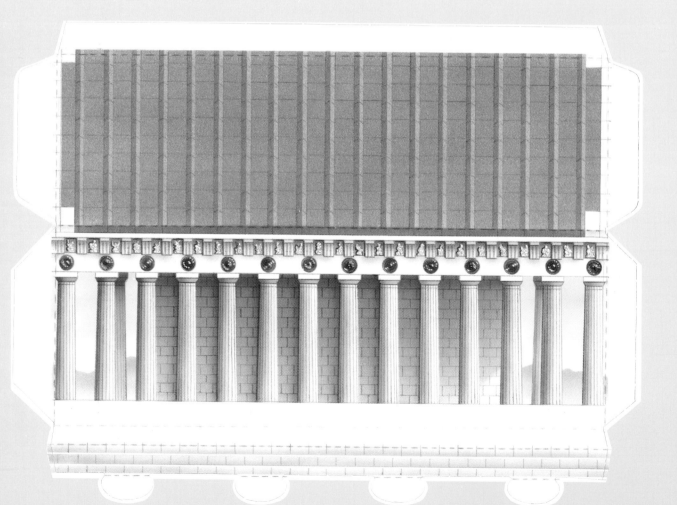

F
F
F
F
F
F
F
F
G
G

4

BACK

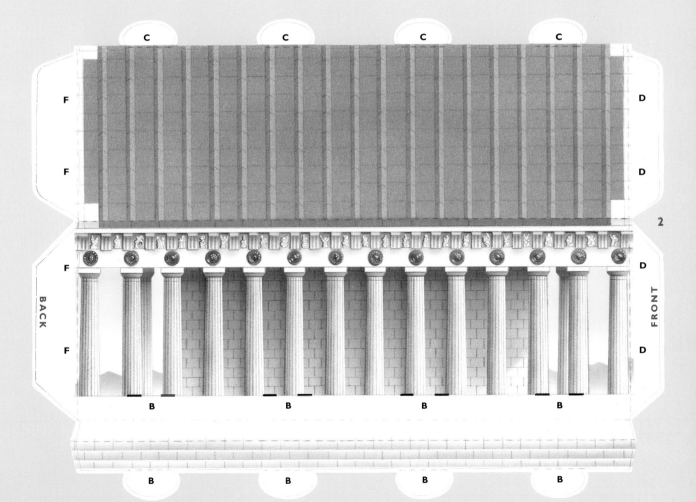

C
C
C
C

F
D

F
D

2

F
D

BACK
FRONT

F
D

B
B
B
B

B
B
B
B

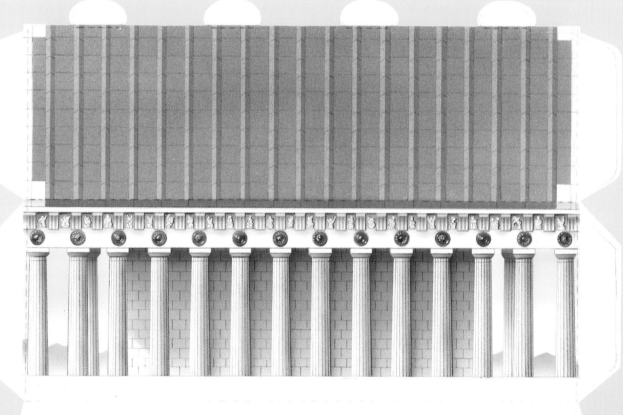

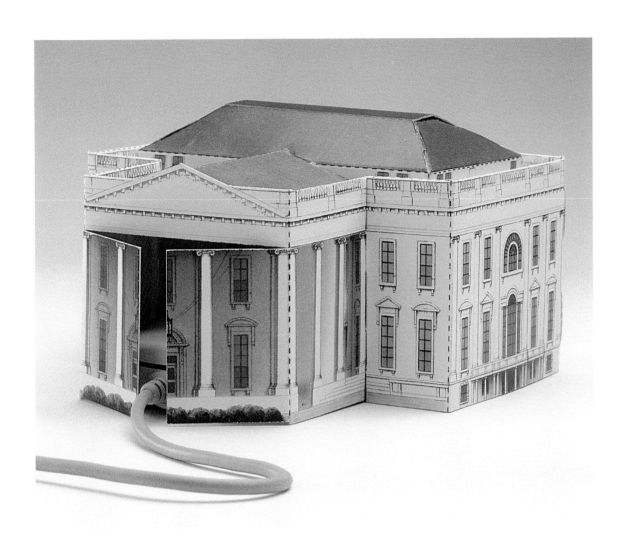

The White House

The mouse with a taste for power need look no further than 1600 Pennsylvania Avenue. Built in 1792, the historic White House, with its seven bedrooms, six bathrooms, and one oval office, has been home to generations of distinguished American mice. Convenient location offers easy access to public transportation. Tax-free, by special arrangement with the American people.

PIECE 1 (entrance): Fold away from you along all dotted score lines, except uppermost panels AA. Fold these panels towards you. (Make sure the upper "railing" panels are folded back and straight down to form two-sided rails; burnish the folds with your thumbnail to keep the rails flat.)

PIECE 2 (front and side walls): Fold away from you along all dotted score lines, except panels AA. Connect piece 1 to piece 2 using tabs A to slots A. Tuck tab B under the folded railing of piece 1. **HINT**: Look at the shape of the roof piece 9—it provides a good floor plan for assembling the walls.

PIECE 3 (rear wall): Fold rounded piece on its two dotted score lines so that rectangular part stands up and semicircular part is perpendicular to wall. Fold away from you along all other dotted score lines, except panels AA. Connect piece 3 to piece 2 using tabs C to slots C.

PIECE 4 (front and side walls): Fold as you did for piece 2. Connect piece 4 to piece 3 by inserting tabs D into slots D. Do not connect piece 1 to piece 4 yet.

PIECE 5 (rear portico): Bend into half circle. (Rolling piece around toilet paper tube or another cylinder is helpful.) Insert tabs G into vertical slots G in center of piece 3. Tuck tabs H under folded railings of piece 3. Push rounded piece at bottom of piece 3 up and into bottom of portico to brace its curve.

PIECE 6 (peaked roof): Fold away from you along all dotted score lines. Then insert tabs I, J, K, and L into corresponding slots I, J, K, and L. Tape tabs N to inside of walls to form corners. Reinforce all tabs with tape on underside.

PIECE 7 (octagon): Fold away from you along all dotted score lines. The side rectangles make little walls supporting the octagonal roof. Insert tab O into slot O on back of piece 6.

PIECE 8 (entrance peaked roof): Fold away from you along all dotted score lines. Insert tabs Q into slots Q on front of piece 6.

PIECE 9 (flat roof): Fold away from you along all dotted score lines. Connect upper roof assembly (pieces 6, 7, and 8) to piece 9 by inserting tabs P, R, and S into corresponding slots P, R, and S. Make sure that the rectangular tabs on piece 7 stay folded under octagonal roof. Now insert tabs T and U that encircle piece 9 into corresponding slots T and U below railing. Start at the front of the building and work your way around, counterclockwise, taping tabs on backside as you go. Connect piece 1 and piece 4 by inserting tabs E and F into slots E and F.

PUT MOUSE IN HOUSE.

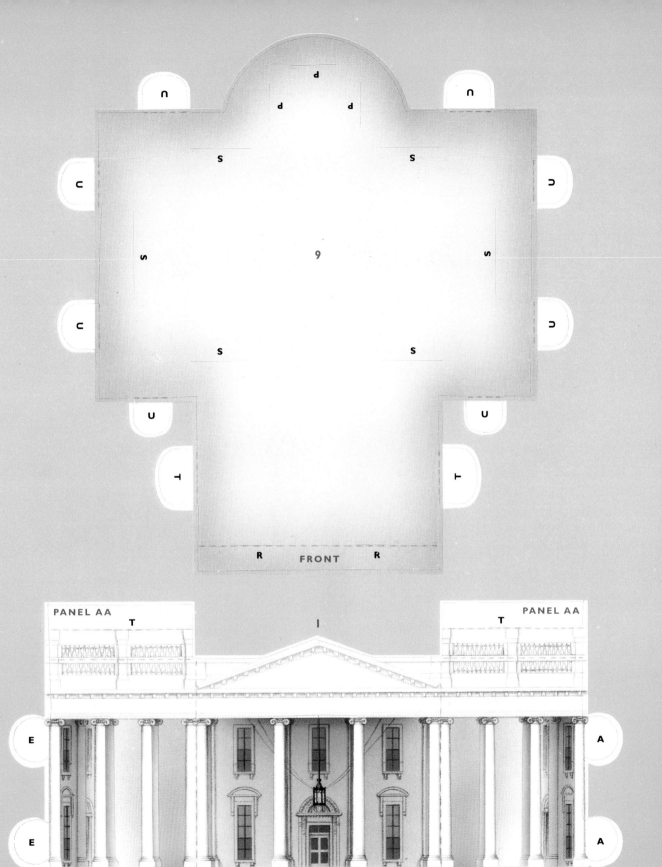

PANEL AA

PANEL AA

FRONT

FRONT

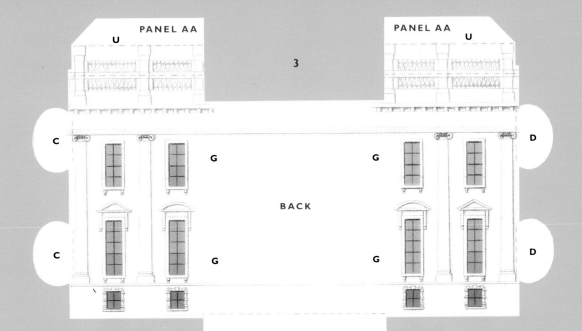

PANEL AA

PANEL AA

3

U

U

C

D

G

G

BACK

C

D

G

G

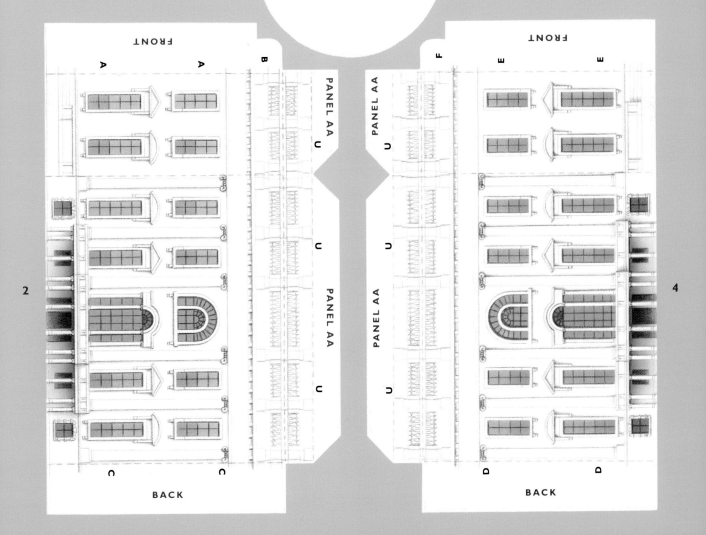

FRONT

FRONT

A

A

E

E

B

F

PANEL AA

PANEL AA

U

U

2

4

PANEL AA

PANEL AA

U

U

U

U

U

D

D

BACK

BACK

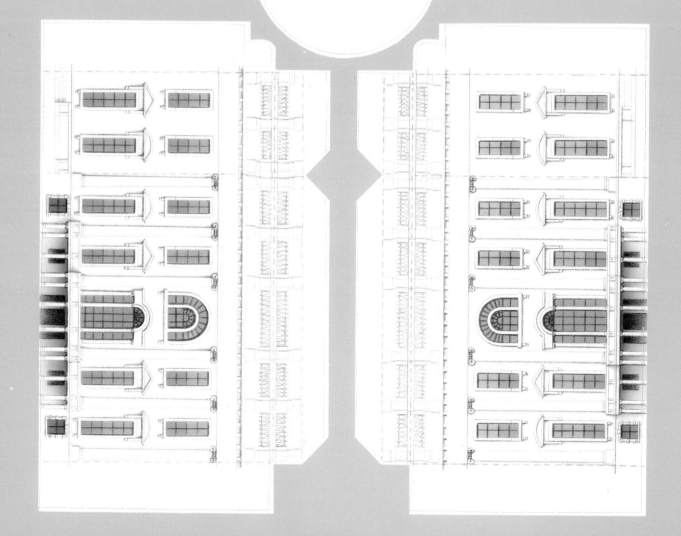

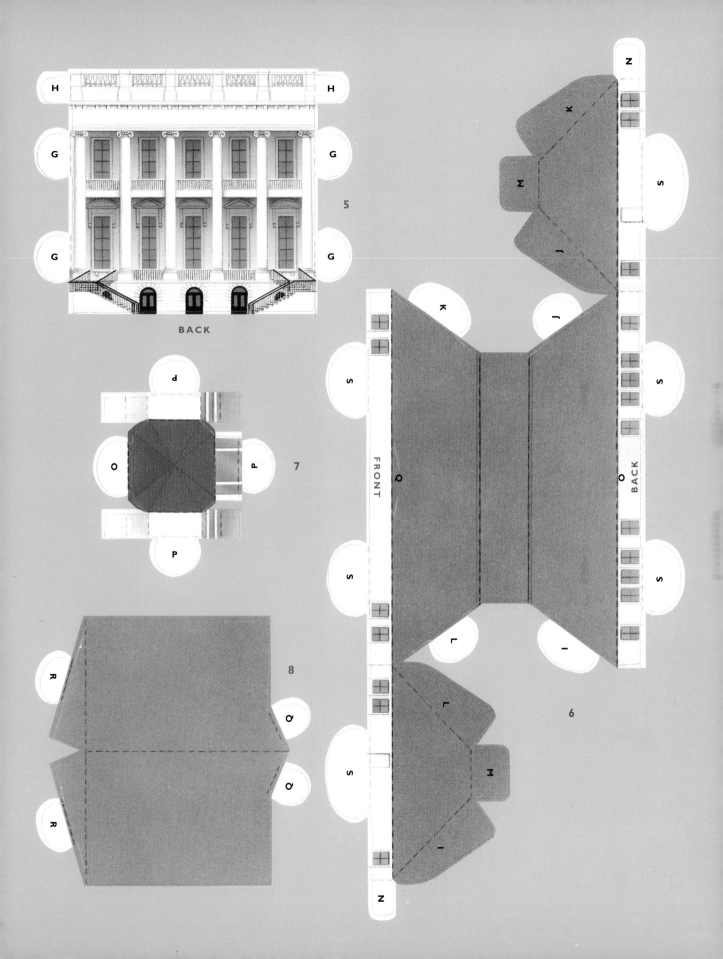

BACK

5

7

8

FRONT

BACK

6

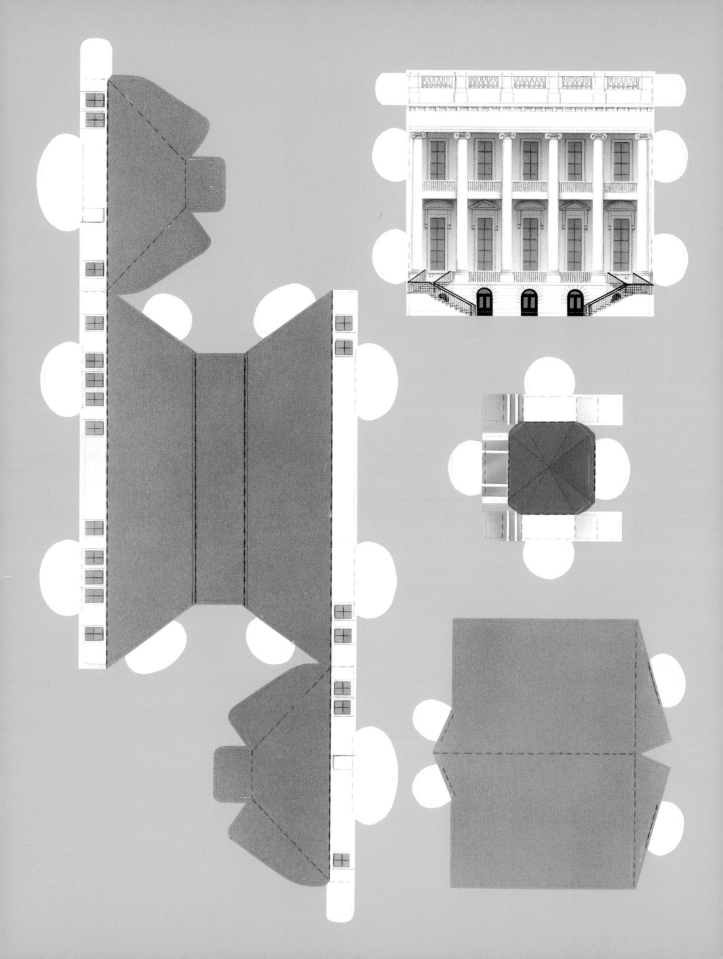

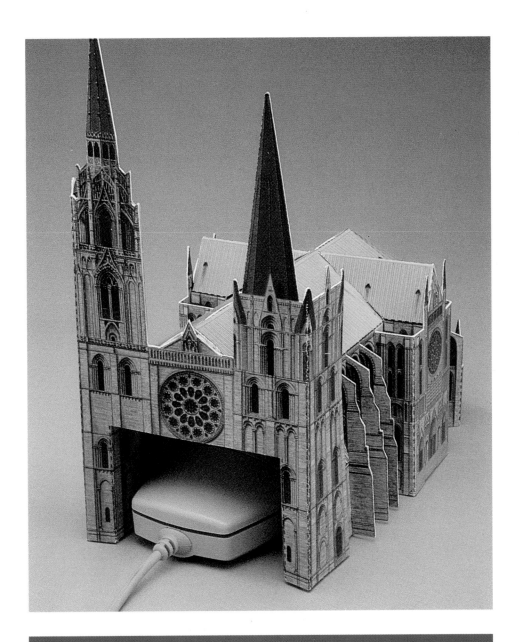

Chartres Cathedral

Who wouldn't love to be the proud resident of a medieval masterpiece? Your mouse will adore this peaceful residence, with its vaulted ceilings, excellent detail work, and spectacular stained glass windows. Vast central chamber, with pew seating, ideal for formal entertaining. Candles not included.

Outside, two 350-foot-high spires frame a unique and stunning entrance. Includes two acres of riverfront property along the historic Eure River, suitable for guest cottage or boathouse.

PIECE 1 (side wall): Fold green roof and narrow panels that border roof away from you along dotted score lines. Fold away from you along all other score lines. Insert tab A into slot A.

PIECE 2 (side wall): Fold along same dotted score lines as you did for piece 1. Insert tab B into slot B. Connect roof halves by inserting tabs C, D, and E into corresponding slots. Bend semicircular roof section to form conical dome for cathedral apse. Insert tab F into slot F. Secure all tabs on underside.

PIECE 3 (apse wall): Form piece into a semicircle. (Rolling it around a toilet paper tube or other cylinder is helpful.) Connect to back ends of wall, inserting tabs G into slots G. Secure with tape on underside. Tape multiple tabs of apse dome to inside of piece 3, being careful not to tape over slots in wall. Be sure that top of apse wall lines up with bottom edge of apse roof.

PIECE 4 (side entrances): Fold all dotted score lines, including tabs, away from you. Align slots H at ends of long center brace with slots H at rear of side walls. Push upwards. Insert tabs I into slots I. Insert tabs J into bottom brace slots J. Connect remaining side tabs K to cathedral roof slots K. Fold panel L at bottom of center brace back towards apse.

PIECE 5 (side roof): Fold all dotted score lines away from you. Join slots M to one another. Insert piece into top of either side entrance, with flaps M facing downwards. Connect tabs N to slots N. Tuck tabs O into peak of side roof.

PIECE 6 (side roof): Repeat what you did for piece 6.

PIECE 7 (low rear wall): Bend this piece around apse and connect to side entrance walls by inserting tabs P into slots P.

PIECES 8-10 (chapels): Fold away from you along all dotted score lines. Push slots Q into corresponding slots Q along top of piece 7. Insert tabs R into slots along apse wall under dome.

PIECES 11-16 (flying buttresses): Attach three to each side of cathedral. Push tabs S into slots at bottom of center segments of side walls. Insert tabs T into vertical slots under roof line.

PIECE 17 (cathedral front): Fold away from you along all dotted score lines. Tuck tabs U into slots formed at peak of cathedral roof. Secure these tabs with tape on the underside. Insert tabs V and W into corresponding slots. Bend these tabs forward on underside and secure with tape. Insert tabs X into bottom brace slots.

PUT MOUSE IN HOUSE.

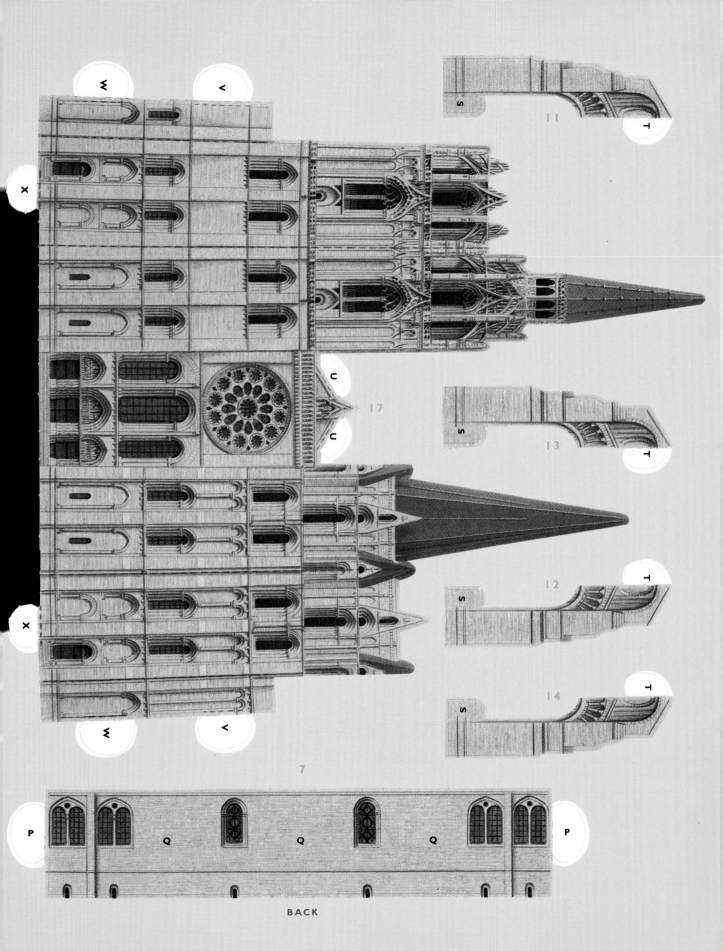

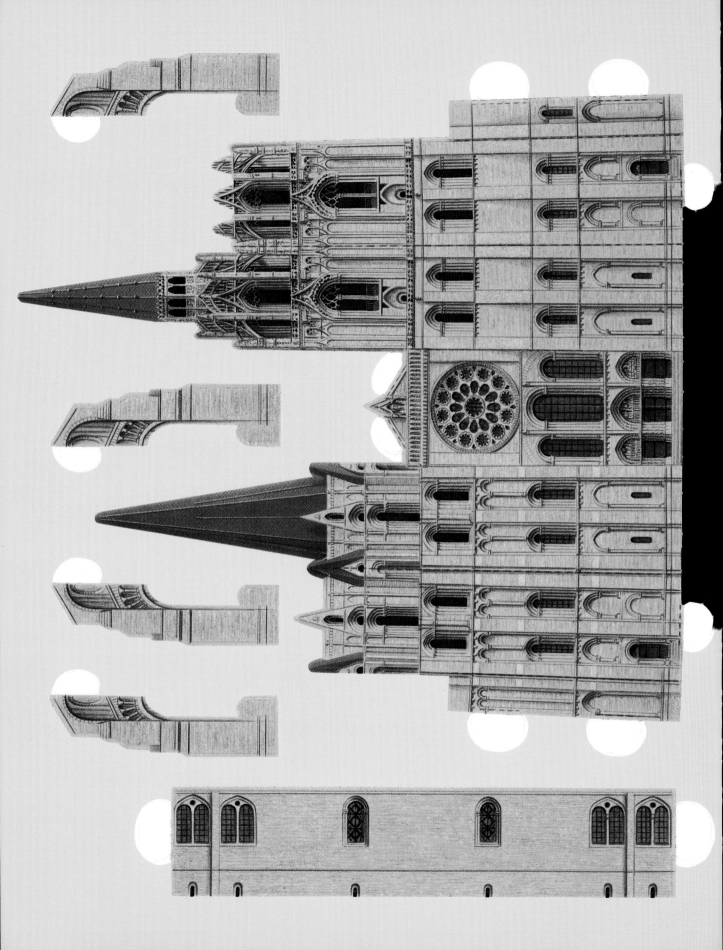

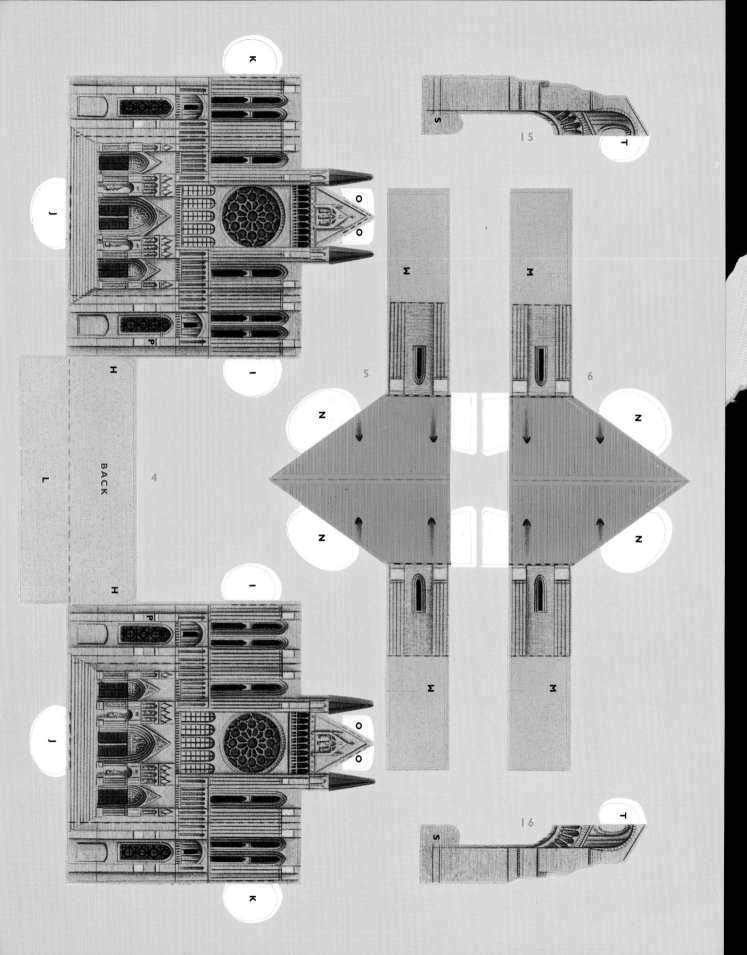

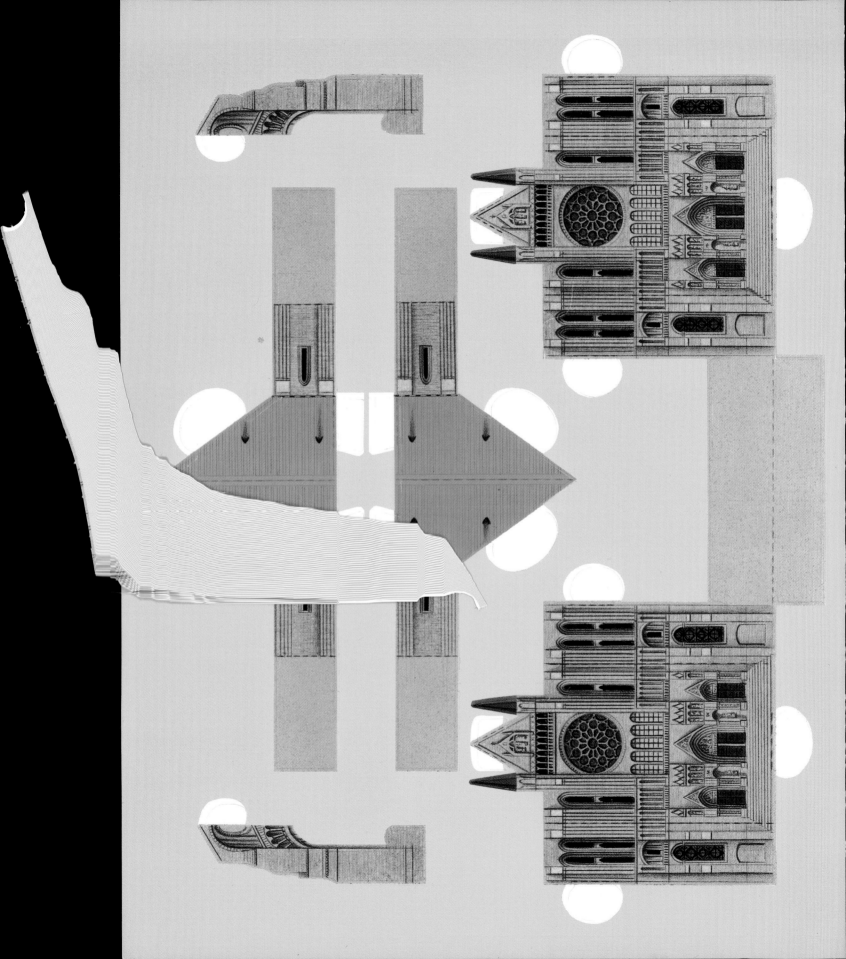

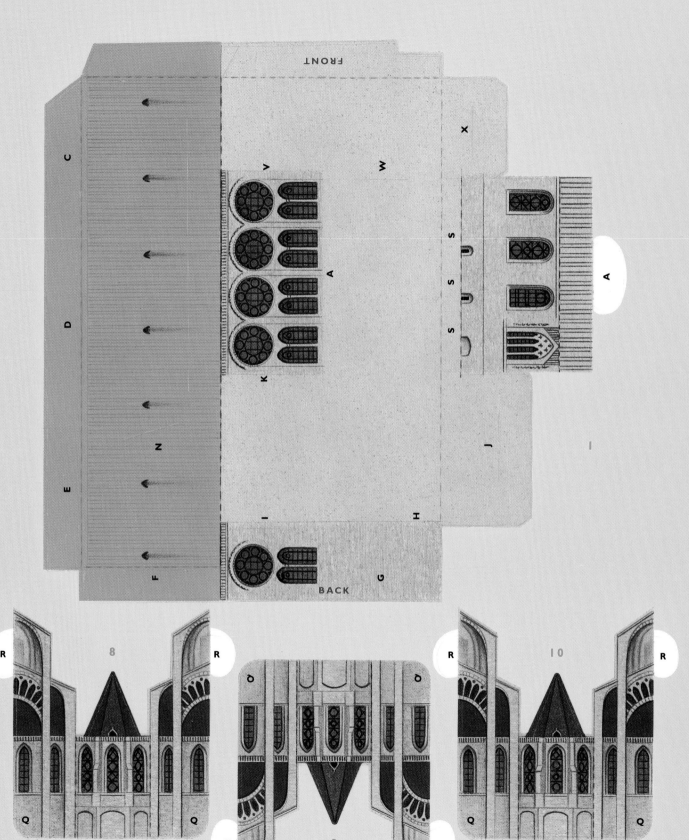

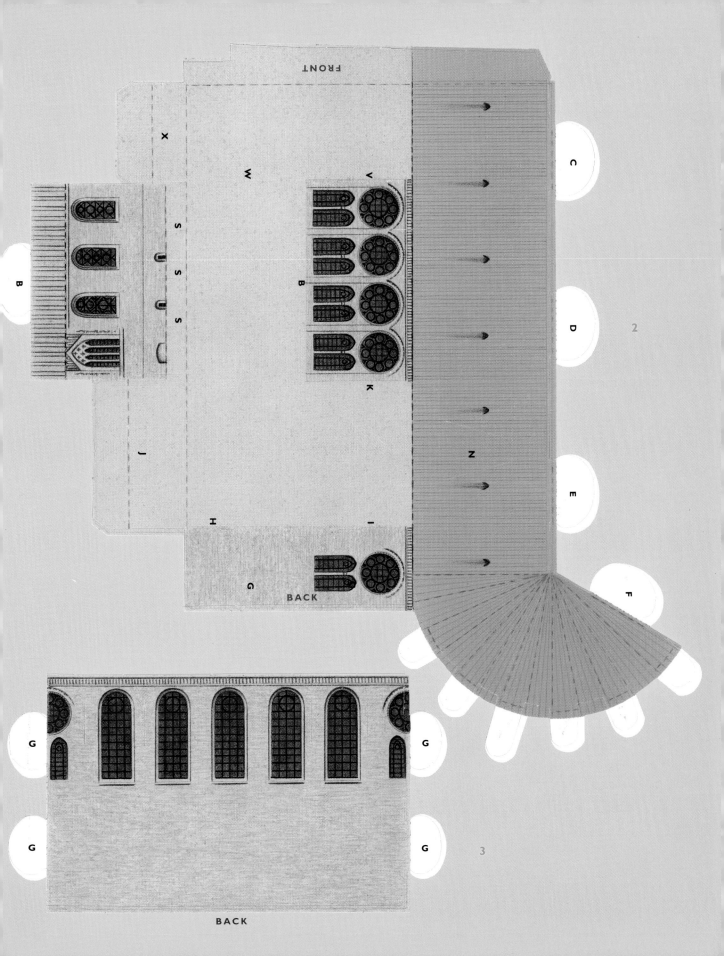